PROACTIVE

ACHIEVING EXCELLENCE IN SALES AND CUSTOMER RELATIONSHIPS

PROACTIVE

ACHIEVING EXCELLENCE IN SALES AND CUSTOMER RELATIONSHIPS

WILL GRAY

© 2021 by Will Gray

All rights reserved. Published 2021.

Printed in the United States of America.

To strive, to seek, to find . . . and not to yield.

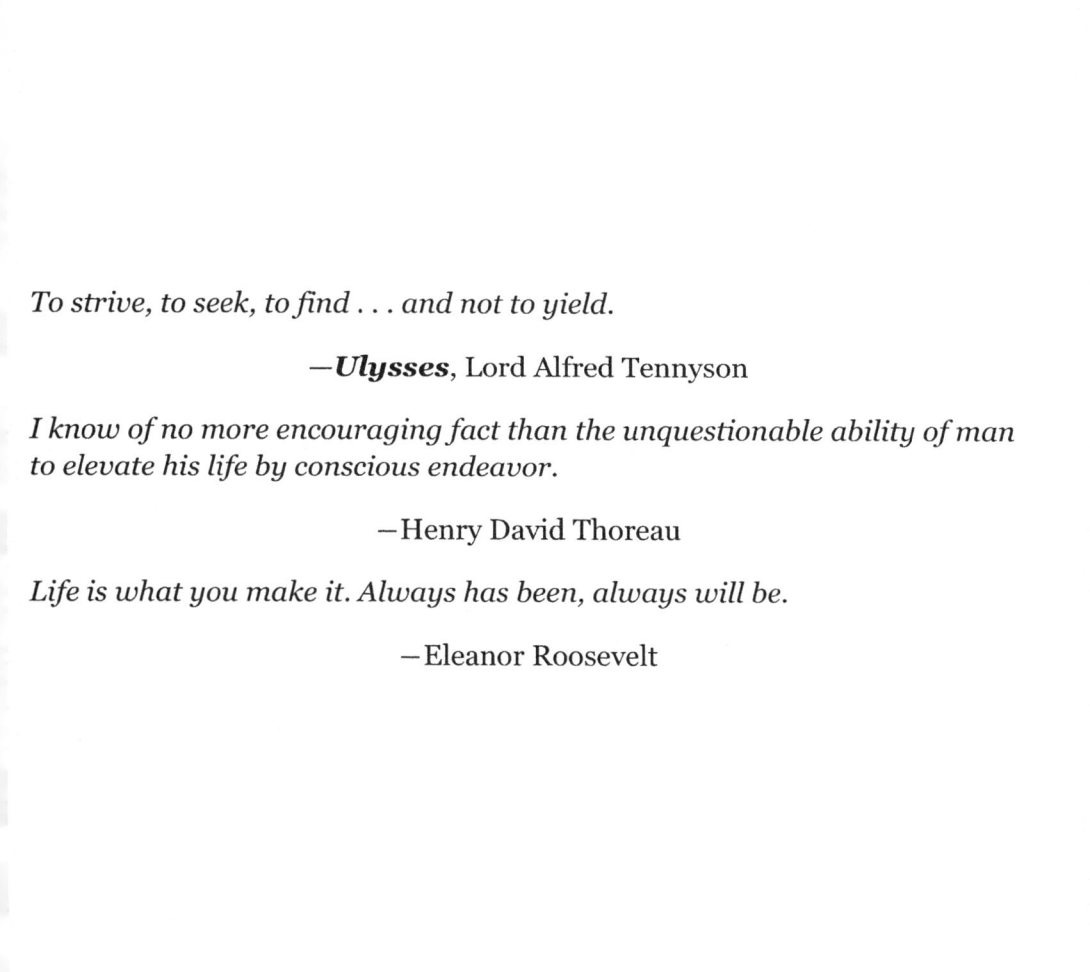

> —***Ulysses***, Lord Alfred Tennyson

I know of no more encouraging fact than the unquestionable ability of man to elevate his life by conscious endeavor.

> —Henry David Thoreau

Life is what you make it. Always has been, always will be.

> —Eleanor Roosevelt

TABLE OF CONTENTS

NOTE FROM THE AUTHOR I

INTRODUCTION I

CHAPTER 1: MENTALITY 4
   What is Your Philosophy? 4
   Accountability 6
   Avoid the Maginot Mentality 7

CHAPTER 2: PLANNING 9
   Develop a Plan: Set Concrete Goals, Measure Progress 9
   Time Management 10
   Quarterly Business Reviews (QBR) 10
   Relevant Topics of Interest 11
   It Begins and Ends with the Customer 12
   Analytics 14
   Mechanics of the QBR 14
      What Not to Do in QBRs 15
   Communication 16

CHAPTER 3: HUMAN CONNECTION 18
   Coaches 18
   3 People 20
   Getting the Call 22
   Stakeholder Engagement 24
   Developing Relationships 25
   Fly Everywhere—Talk to Everyone 26
   Ask For the Business 29
   Seek Feedback 30

CHAPTER 4: EXCELLING 32
   Preparation 32
   Value 33
   Leverage Resources 35
   Thriving In a Virtual Environment 37
   Differentiate 38
   Become the Expert 40

Ideal 41

CHAPTER 5: MAINTAINING THE EDGE 44
Question your Path 44
Would it Matter 46
Mix It Up 46
Anything is Possible 47
Get Uncomfortable 49
Improvise. Adapt. Overcome. 50
Owner 51
Thank-You Notes 52

CHAPTER 6: LEADERSHIP 53
Hard on the Issues, Not the Person 53
Eat Last 54
Will or Won't, Can or Can't 55
Leading By Example 56
That's Thirty Minutes Away, I'll Be There In Ten 57
Hire Slow, Fire Fast 57
Drop Anchors 58

CHAPTER 7: SCENARIOS 60
Keeping Your Best Employees 60
What If They Leave? 61
Saying Goodbye 62
Best Customer Moves or Abandons You 63
Challenging Customers 64
New Entrant In the Market 65
Losing 67

FINAL THOUGHTS 68

ABOUT THE AUTHOR 72

ENDNOTES 73

ACKNOWLEDGMENTS

I would like to thank the amazing friends who selflessly provided countless hours of their time, patience, and perspective to make this book a reality. To Jason Riley, one of the authors of *Left of Bang*. Your friendship and insight have been amazing. Your book gave me the inspiration to start this journey.

To my wife, Amy, and sons Jack and Matt. Thank you for reading and providing feedback. Amy, thanks for always being in my corner and supporting me. You make me a better person.

Thank you to the following people who gave their time and attention to this book with wonderful feedback: Gavin Phillips, Andy Olen, Carolyn Amato, Denis Harrington, Eric Siebert, Mark Dixon, Marc Turner, and to my editors Sarah Mayer and Nadene Seiters.

Larry Muschamp helped inspire this book. My headmaster at Oak Hall School in Gainesville, Florida, he was a charismatic speaker and a wonderful mentor. As a teacher, he ignited my love of history and set me on the path to writing this book.

Thank you to the best salesperson I've ever known, Fred Gongola from Frito-Lay. Fred coached, motivated, and encouraged me. A special thank you to Marc Turner, an incredible leader and an even better person.

I also want to acknowledge my late parents, Henry and Ellen Gray. My mother was a prolific reader with a great sense of style and humor. She always had a twinkle in her eye and raised five kids. Talk about proactive. My father was an amazing man and will always be my role model and hero. Smart, funny, driven, and loving. He was a gifted storyteller, always encouraging and often told me how much he loved me. I was a lucky kid.

NOTE FROM THE AUTHOR

Growing up in the north Florida town of Gainesville—the youngest of five children—I always believed I would be an attorney like my father and his before him. Fascinated by history, I loved the stories about my family and the impact of service to community and country. Sports and the concepts of responsibility, competition, leadership, and camaraderie have always resonated with me.

After serving as an officer on active duty in the Marine Corps, I returned to the University of Florida to earn my MBA full time. It was a transitional time that allowed me to explore various career opportunities. I quickly determined traditional finance and marketing careers held little appeal for me. I thrived on setting and achieving goals and enjoyed working in and leading teams.

The day the recruiters from Frito-Lay PepsiCo came to campus was an epiphany for me. They reminded me of Marines. They weren't wearing suits, they spoke about the challenge of selling, they laughed a lot, and clearly liked each other. They were a team.

The recruiters explained that the new hires for the management program would have to get up at 3 a.m., drive a chip truck, learn how to sell, and fill the shelves at gas stations and grocery stores for four months before being allowed to lead a team. I never considered myself a salesperson, but I thought this would be challenging and fun. Many of my classmates were horrified.

I had an MBA and had served as an officer in the Marines, and now I was driving a chip truck. I loved it.

After a few years of learning how to sell and becoming ingrained in the amazing culture at Frito-Lay, I had an offer to work for a medical device company. Even though the compensation was much higher, I really struggled to leave Frito-Lay. The culture of selling imbued everything we did. Titles and education never mattered. It was the teamwork. It was results. It was the winning spirit.

Having spent the last twenty years and counting at another great company, Boston Scientific, I have worked with talented leaders and observed peers, competitors, and customers who have inspired and molded my sales and leadership styles. I had the fortune of being awarded four President's Clubs early in my career by being proactive and being lucky to work alongside some great people.

For the past decade, I've been put into positions that have exposed me to unique and challenging circumstances that have demanded proactivity. Working with large customers and managing diverse teams has been an amazing learning experience.

This book describes many of the lessons I have learned in my career. Many of the stories represent recollections and experiences over time. Some of the events and details about people have been changed. It is a testament to the talented sales professionals and leaders who have taught me so much; about what to do and what not to do.

INTRODUCTION

Whether on the streets of Mogadishu, Somalia or in the boardrooms of Wall Street, life has a way of humbling you when you aren't prepared.

You have a meeting with a big client, and your computer won't turn on.

You oversleep before the final interview.

The competition takes your biggest customer to dinner at your favorite restaurant.

Your top-producing sales representative resigns.

Life is full of twists and turns.

Life is also full of choices. How you choose to live your life, treat people, engage with customers, and manage your business all comes down to a choice. There are roadblocks and catalysts along the way. But remember, how you react is a choice. Choose wisely.

Introduction

Those that are proactive and determine where to best guide their ship will stay ahead of the competition. By constantly questioning your path and looking for ways to improve, people and companies can thrive. If you are reacting to events beyond your control, you become defensive and less effective.

I don't define winning by economic gain, title, or so-called societal status. It doesn't matter how much money you make or where you live. For me, success entails becoming the person you want to be by fulfilling your passions, treating others how you want to be treated, and becoming the best version of yourself.

History is full of examples where people and companies lost everything because they failed to plan.

Innovations throughout history have transformed society. The mass production of the Model T Ford in the early 1900s challenged the horse and buggy; enhancements to steel production drove the industrial revolution and virtually eliminated the market for handcrafts; and the invention of the personal computer eventually sent typewriters and VCRs into obsolescence.

Email allows millions of people to communicate instantly, regardless of location or time of day. The advent of Amazon, Federal Express, and UPS has driven the post office to the brink of collapse.

Uber, the iPhone, and Airbnb—why didn't the companies that owned the predicate technologies and services prepare? Why didn't the taxi industry, Blackberry, and hotel chains understand the transformative nature of these disruptions to the status quo?

They were complacent and failed to be proactive.

What happens when your best customer stops returning your phone calls or you receive terse email responses? That has happened to me many times. That voice in your head tells you something is wrong.

The business world rewards those who can read the environment, prepare for any eventuality, and maximize value for themselves and their clients.

Introduction

This book is about taking a disciplined approach in your planning and execution to ensure success. It is for the business leader looking to grow their company to new heights or the established firm trying to reinvent itself and strive for greatness. It is for the sales professional and the sales leader searching for ways to create value beyond product and price. Being proactive will accelerate your performance.

CHAPTER 1: MENTALITY

Complacency is the enemy of greatness.

In business, understanding the environment and noticing changes in the social landscape will help you minimize threats. Flexibility and continual diligence can enhance readiness and ensure you thrive in challenging circumstances. Proactively interacting with customers and your peers will strengthen your position.

How can we ensure we persevere and advance in business?

WHAT IS YOUR PHILOSOPHY?

Whether building a new team, replacing a great employee, or deciding how to answer a tough customer question, your decision-making is critical. If you don't have a philosophy, it's time to create one. The philosophy should be consistent, and it should focus on making the team and you better.

That philosophy should include, at a minimum, the following: be positive and encouraging, challenge the status quo, focus on improvement, and hire and promote driven, positive people.

Don't blame the situation, your team, or others when things go wrong. Take responsibility for the issue and proactively focus on a solution and getting better.

The leader who looks for ways to improve while celebrating successes is a rare individual.

One of the best leaders I ever worked for was a tough Marine officer who had high standards and was a renaissance man. He was a voracious reader of nonfiction and focused on nontraditional aspects of military doctrine, like supply and logistics. His philosophy was centered on a belief that self and organizational improvement must be embraced on a daily basis.

He asked for ideas and feedback from younger officers, which really didn't happen much thirty years ago. He was constantly trying to improve his team, his unit, and himself. He was also willing to ask for help from others if he couldn't figure it out. He let go of his ego. What a rare quality in the military and civilian worlds.

If you don't have a philosophy people can identify with and that resonates, it is time to create one. Go through a discovery process and create a mission or purpose statement and values. Consider your purpose and how you want to treat each other and your customers. Determine the ideal traits of the people you want on the team, and then identify what success looks like and empower critical behaviors.

Here are some examples of great mission statements:

- Nordstrom: "In our store or online, wherever new opportunities arise—Nordstrom works relentlessly to give customers the most compelling shopping experience possible. The one constant? John W. Nordstrom's founding philosophy: offer the customer the best possible service, selection, quality and value.[i]

- Amazon: "To be Earth's most customer-centric company."[ii]
- The mission of The Walt Disney Company is "to entertain, inform and inspire people around the globe through the power of unparalleled storytelling, reflecting the iconic brands, creative minds and innovative technologies that make ours the world's premier entertainment company."[iii]

Values are those core beliefs that set the foundation of the company. They should define the company and be a guiding light for employees. They create a common sense of purpose and should always be adhered to.[iv] Here are some examples:

- Marriott: Put People First, Pursue excellence, Act with integrity, Embrace change and Serve our world[v]
- Kellogg's: Integrity, accountability, passion, humility, simplicity, results[vi]
- Salesforce: Trust, customer success, innovation, equality[vii]
- CB Insights: Hard work, High Standards, Hunger, Helpfulness, Humility[viii]
- CampMinder: Put team first, Own it, Be admirable, Wonder, Find a Better Way, Give joy[ix]

ACCOUNTABILITY

Leaders who embrace accountability are usually very successful.

Accountability means focusing on your responsibilities and holding your team and yourself to your commitments. This task takes discipline. At the end of the day, ask yourself if you are doing everything you can to accomplish the objective.

There is a leader I know who truly differentiates himself by his incredible drive and passion to be great. His work effort is amazing, and his team and organization know it. His direct reports often comment he is tough to work for, but he always delivers on commitments and rewards great performance. If you need help, he is there. It takes a unique organization to accept someone with such drive, and he is successful. Every person who knows him has the same reaction when his name is brought up; they laugh. They laugh because he is so driven and motivated, he accomplishes things through force of character and personality. He is different. While that type of leadership isn't for everyone, he is accountable and always proactively shapes the environment.

Accountability breeds success, and those who focus on it will win. But be mindful that this type of approach may be new and jarring to some. You don't need to drive people away with it, but also keep in mind those who don't embrace accountability may not be a good fit with an organization that relies on it.

AVOID THE MAGINOT MENTALITY

Lacking proactivity means embracing complacency. Doing things the way they have always been done or being defensive often leads to failure.

After emerging victorious in WWI—although with deep emotional and physical scars from the devastating effects of war—France embarked on a journey of rebuilding itself and its military after the 1919 signing of the Versailles Treaty. In the 1930s French leaders Marshal Petain and Charles De Gaulle argued for two different approaches to the repair and rebuilding of the military. Petain's plan won with the support of French Prime Minister Clemenceau, and France built a seemingly impregnable line of fortifications, weapons, and obstacles. This line stretched the length of the French border to Italy, Germany, Switzerland, and Luxembourg. It was based on the premise that in trench warfare like WWI, the Germans would become bottled up and the French could mobilize and counterattack. French military experts believed the fortifications were impenetrable and boasted of their strength. The Maginot Line ultimately constituted a large, long, fortified trench between France and her potential enemies.

The Germans developed a bold plan to bypass the Maginot Line—they simply went around it—by streaming through the Low Countries (Belgium, Luxembourg, and the Netherlands) and into France in May of 1940. Within six weeks, the Germans were in Paris. A week later, France was suing for peace and became nothing more than a resisting force for the next five years of WWII.

The French had more than twenty years to formulate their plan for the defense of their country, and Petain's plan was never seriously questioned. Even during the invasion of Poland in September 1939, when Germany's blitzkrieg strategy revealed itself, why didn't someone question the Maginot Line?

This "Maginot mentality" spread across France as the leaders and citizens became defensive in their thinking and approach to national security.[x] Their relations with other countries also suffered as France focused on their own survival and avoidance of conflict.

This type of Maginot mentality occurs all the time in business. Companies build business plans focused on what the competition will do instead of creating bold strategies to differentiate themselves. Many companies also have leaders who refuse to listen to constructive criticism or new ideas from junior employees. They lack flexibility and are not proactive. Don't have the Maginot mentality.

Innovate, differentiate. Measure what matters.

CHAPTER 2: PLANNING

DEVELOP A PLAN: SET CONCRETE GOALS, MEASURE PROGRESS

Planning is a critical component of proactivity. The key to an effective business plan is the creation of meaningful, quantifiable goals. Measure progress toward goal accomplishment and provide regular updates. The plan must be dynamic in that it is updated in real time. Don't waste your time on obsolete goals, or ones you can't measure progress toward.[xi]

Setting meaningful goals is hard. Real hard. Having the discipline to include others in the process and gain consensus takes time, hard work, and deep thinking. But it is worth it. Because when you have shared and measurable objectives, they become a compass for your journey.

They should also be aggressive but achievable, and they should be accomplished within a quarter.

While many companies have inspirational, talented founders and CEOs with amazing visions, they often lack management muscle and discipline. Teams need a template for success and goals that create alignment, clarity and engagement.

The goals should be SMART:[xii]

- Specific
- Measurable
- Actionable
- Realistic
- Time-Bound

Business plans are important because they keep you focused on what matters, and they drive accountability when you use them appropriately. Review them weekly and make sure they are fresh and relevant.

TIME MANAGEMENT

I know. I know. Managing your time is hard work. It takes discipline. Few have the grit to do it on a regular basis. I struggle with it.

We get caught up in the minutiae of our personal and business lives and forget what we were working on an hour ago, much less a week ago.

Stay focused on what really matters. Be proactive.

Do it now. Adopt Microsoft Notes or another platform and organize your thoughts and your priorities and make it a part of your routine. Set aside fifteen minutes daily in your calendar to manage these priorities and have the discipline to stick to that routine. You will quickly find you become much more efficient and effective.

QUARTERLY BUSINESS REVIEWS (QBR)

A QBR—Quarterly Business Review—is a face-to-face meeting with the customer and aligned internal stakeholders to review performance and priorities.

The QBR should always be tailored to the customer and their priorities. This is an excellent opportunity to engage with customers on a routine basis and reinforce your relationship, your mutual priorities, and the strength of your portfolio or service.

One of the most critical components of the QBR is a review of quarterly and annual sales results, ideally comparing them to the prior period to look at trends and areas of opportunity. If the relationship is based on something beyond revenue, like a service commitment, then use the most relevant factors as the focus of the review. This is the time to identify what is going well and how things can be improved. An important aspect of the QBR is it should have some key takeaways and measurable follow-up items.

RELEVANT TOPICS OF INTEREST

This is an often-overlooked aspect of a QBR. Perform research to identify market changes, customer news, and the competitive landscape to show the customer you have prepared and the meeting is important. It also builds your credibility, which is critical to the strength of a business relationship.

Likeability helps, but ultimately, your customer needs to respect you and believe you can deliver what you are offering. Perform research on the customer (including their work experience and educational background) and attempt to find special interests or accomplishments you can bring up during discussions. If he is a clinician, explore recent topics affecting their specialty, like recent clinical trial releases or changes to reimbursement. If he is in finance, identify significant trends in the stock market. One of my favorite approaches is identifying something interesting about their hometown or alma mater.

As you get to know the customer, take notes in order to remember the important aspects of your conversations so you can refer to them in the next meeting. It takes a tremendous amount of discipline, but it is amazing how few people do it because it is a true differentiator. It keeps you proactive.

Doing research and fully understanding what potential experiences or passions the customer has always makes it easier to get the conversation flowing. Identify mutual acquaintances and reach out to them to understand the client's style, preferences, and topics to stay away from.

Send handwritten thank-you notes after a meeting—a personal touch that never disappoints.

IT BEGINS AND ENDS WITH THE CUSTOMER

The customer matters. Yes, it's true.

Never give a presentation focused on your priorities. Always place the interests of the client first. Please.

Human nature indicates people care mostly about their own thoughts and priorities, and so every presentation should begin and end with the customer in mind.

We sat down at the table and greeted the customer who appeared to be having a very long day. She was famous—or notorious—for having very little patience for inane chatter. She had a job and didn't want to focus on anything but business. When my peer opened his computer and asked for the cord for the overhead, she simply said "no". When he asked her what she meant, she stated she was sick of these canned presentations about products she didn't understand. Don't waste my time, she said. I have a fixed budget, and at this rate, I am going to exceed it by 10 percent, and I don't need to hear about your new expensive products.

We left the discussion feeling crushed. In hindsight, the customer was crying out for help.

We lost an opportunity to learn about the customer. What we should have done is conducted research beforehand on the customer and her challenges and opportunities. What was important to her? Then, we should have tailored the presentation and our focus on alignment with her goals.

Start with the priorities of the customer and determine their stated or implied goals and keys to success. In healthcare, a customer's priorities can include better outcomes, the cost of care, employee engagement, and patient satisfaction. In consumer products, priorities include margin, inventory management, service, and customer satisfaction. The key is understanding what is important to the customer and framing your conversation around their priorities and challenges. This can be discovered on the client's website under priorities, values, and mission, or you can simply ask them.

Next, identify where the customer and you have common ground. Where do you have similar objectives and interests? Write them down and gain agreement from the customer that there are synergies to working together to accomplish common objectives.

Then, develop a plan of action. Since you have already agreed on mutual interests, discuss how a partnership (contract) can lead to a mutual achievement of goals. [xiii]

An example of how to keep the customer at the forefront is a discussion between a supplier and a customer who had historically struggled to maintain a positive relationship. In doing research, the supplier identified that one of the strategic imperatives of the customer was to reduce customer wait times because it was adversely affecting patient care and patient satisfaction.

In the initial meeting, the supplier showed a quote from the customer CEO expressing a desire to decrease customer wait times. The customer was impressed the supplier had quoted the CEO and acknowledged it was at the top of his list personally. He even showed a scorecard used to assess his performance, and this metric was at the top. Do you think he was interested in this conversation? I do.

The supplier then showed him a quote from the supplier's chief technology officer that the company had recently launched a unique technology which had proven in a study to reduce customer wait times significantly through digital tools.

There was clearly a need for the customer to adopt the technology, and they subsequently collaborated on a contract with agreeable terms. They also scheduled a regular cadence of performance reviews to ensure alignment on desired outcomes. This scenario resulted in a new type of customer relationship where trust was created through value creation and shared interests.

Another important component of customer engagement is being able to read the room. Look at the customer's body language and always start the meeting with expectations for the discussion. Ask the customer if the time allotted still works and if there is anything specifically they want to address in the beginning of the meeting. This approach really works!

ANALYTICS

A critical part of performing the Quarterly Business Review is ensuring you have the numbers to reinforce your value. Analytics refers to the analysis of data to show the financial impact of your offer. It could be a cost benefit, revenue growth, or a margin analysis.

You must quantify the benefit of the product or service that you are providing. The analysis should also be impactful, visual, simple, and repeatable.

If you are providing invoice savings, use those. If there are rebates, calculate them and illustrate the overall benefit to the customer.

Numbers can be magic.

That is not to say numbers are the only thing that matters. The customer often considers other important factors like product performance, service, relationships, and convenience.

However, analytics allow you to provide unbiased, quantifiable value and mitigate qualitative factors that could influence a buying decision. They are a great way to proactively influence the buying landscape.

MECHANICS OF THE QBR

At the beginning of every QBR, a checklist of deliverables from the previous meeting should be reviewed. This process will highlight the goals achieved and identify the opportunities still outstanding. A healthy discussion should then commence on how to best achieve the outstanding objectives.

After everything is reviewed, the supplier should recap all the deliverables and opportunities once again while ensuring the customer has time to ask questions and agree on next steps.

Some examples of deliverables include a revenue or share commitment, removal of the competition, promotions or discounts on products and services, or adoption of new technology.

Ultimately, you should have a plan and make sure your customer has a voice before, during, and after the QBR. By ensuring a review of objectives and agreement on deliverables and next steps, you will maximize the time and effort of every participant in the process.

WHAT NOT TO DO IN QBRS

QBR No-No's:

Don't:

- Bring too many people. The more people present, the less customers will talk.
- Bring people in who don't understand the current situation and potential roadblocks.
- Give a pipeline presentation (update on current and future products). Just don't do it. Nobody cares.
- Come without a solid plan. Remember to begin with the customer in mind.
- Start the meeting by taking the initiative and talking about yourself and your company.
- Come on a tight schedule. I have seen executives leave in the middle of a meeting. Not good.
- Forget to do check-ins during the meeting with the customer. Make sure they are following along with you and they agree with the direction of the meeting.

- Leave your listening ears at home. Talk much less than you listen.

COMMUNICATION

One of the key components to proactivity is communicating succinctly and frequently with your internal and external customers. By keeping the communication current and by coordinating activities, you can ensure you are positively influencing the environment.

The analogy to the military is very apropos. The concept of proactivity includes the notion that when you face a challenge, it is critical you have a thorough plan for communication with a back-up in case one mode of communication fails (as it inevitably will). Consider a military vehicle hitting an Improvised Explosive Device (IED) and its communications platform being disabled. Then what? That vehicle will have a back-up portable radio, and the occupants will potentially have cell phones. In addition, the other vehicles in the patrol will have several communications platforms at their disposal. There may be helicopters and airplanes nearby that have visual and audio contact with the unit. The command post in the rear at the main base will also have a significant number of communications capabilities they can leverage to identify threats and opportunities to aid and coordinate activities.[xiv]

In the business world, communication comes in all forms: phone calls, conference calls, email, business meetings, and live discussions. The key to proactivity is to manage this communication so all stakeholders are properly informed and the facts and recommendations are properly articulated.

Have you ever walked into a business meeting and the customer tells you they are breaking the contract early? Uh-oh. To mitigate the likelihood this poor outcome will occur, perform Quarterly Business Reviews (QBRs). Communicate to your internal customers on a regular basis that one of the potential outcomes with this customer is that they will break the contract early. Have several questions prepared to ask when they announce the news.

Once the meeting ends, immediately inform the people in your network and begin collaborating on the best approach. Follow up with the customer to see what other potential avenues are available. Refuse to accept defeat.

Another way to influence the environment is to proactively patrol. Patrols—or groups of Marines or soldiers —walk or drive through areas of operations at different times, from different directions, with different levels of force, to keep the enemy off balance. This random movement mitigates the enemy's ability to create a solid plan and mass their forces. It is what I experienced firsthand in Somalia, both as Marines set out on foot and in mechanized vehicles, patrolling at all hours of the day, to keep the enemy from coordinating activities in any meaningful way.

The concept of patrolling works well in sales and relationship management.

Make sure you are checking in with your customer at different times and with different modes of communication. Consistent, impactful communication is essential.

If you are in retail, meet with customers on the sales floor. Ask them about their experience. Study the competition and see how they are differentiating themselves. Send emails, make phone calls, and visit your customers face to face. Utilize digital marketing channels—websites and emails campaigns—to engage customers and receive feedback.

No matter the industry, reach out to your customers for random check-ins. Ask them about your performance and how they believe your product or service is doing. Send them a personalized card on their birthday. Call them and ask them if there is anything you can do to improve your service. Be proactive.

CHAPTER 3: HUMAN CONNECTION

COACHES

One of the best ways to ensure you are being proactive in business and life is by identifying and working with coaches.

In business, a coach is a customer who provides insights and advice to assist you in advancing your position. Coaches can come from many different parts of the customer organization. It could be a secretary or the CEO of the company. Typically, the coach has a vested interest in seeing you or your company succeed. They may have a long-term relationship with you, or perhaps your product or services match their interests the best. They may just believe in your company.

Coaches show you how to find the answers to the questions.

You should attempt to identify a person(s) in the organization who can get you critical information or has access to the people who have the information.

I had a customer that we could never win a deal with. No matter how hard we tried or how much we gave to the customer, they always went with the competition. We brought new people in, gave them additional value, tried to reason and even appeal to their sensitivities. Nothing mattered.

We eventually learned that one of their executives had a relative working for the competition. Pretty good coach, huh? Who do you think had an advantage?

Coaches also exist outside of the business world.

President Richard Nixon resigned on August 8, 1973, a mere month after the Supreme Court ruled all White House tapes concerning Watergate must be turned over. The tapes contained incontrovertible proof Nixon had obstructed justice by ordering the CIA to hinder the FBI's investigation.

Watergate likely would have never become such a major political firestorm resulting in forty convictions if young *Washington Post* reporters Carl Bernstein and Bob Woodward hadn't had the information and coaching from the FBI's second-in-command Mark Felt. Felt spoke or met with Woodward seventeen times over the course of the Watergate ordeal, providing critical information allowing the scandal to grow out of control.[xv]

There are coaches in all walks of life. For anyone who has ever played sports, coaches usually are unforgettable. Next to a parent, coaches are often credited as the biggest influences on peoples' lives. John Wooden, Bill Belicheck, Dawn Staley, Eddie Robinson, and Pat Summitt are a few of the legends that come to mind. They possess a tremendous combination of experience, drive, and knowledge to get results.

Think of all the political candidates who have benefitted from coaches: Bill Clinton and James Carville, George Bush and Karl Rove, Barack Obama and David Axelrod.

In late 2005, US military strategy in Iraq consisted of essentially handing the battle over to the Iraqi Army while US forces stayed mainly in heavily fortified bases. When there was an attack on Iraqi troops, the US military would send a quick reaction force to help.

When the detonation of Improvised Explosive Devices (IEDs) and killings of US military personnel, Iraqi soldiers, and civilians spiraled out of control in the next year, it was the concept of coaching that turned the tide for the Iraqi Army and US forces. The coaching came not only from small numbers of embedded US military advisors in large Iraqi army units but also from the Iraqi citizens who coached the Iraqi military on where the bombs and terrorists were.

When the Americans and Iraqis were able to get the local population to believe in the strength of Iraqi soldiers, the tide of the war turned in favor of the Iraqi military.[xvi]

In business, when you are developing relationships, it is important to identify someone within the organization who can provide key insights and a perspective to help you navigate the complexity of the situation.

Similarly, you need a sales force developing relationships with customers if you're going to identify coaches to convert or retain business. The sales team serves as a connection between the customer and the company through educating the customer on the benefits of the products or services. Through this education, coaches within the customer organization are identified. The relationship with the coach is nurtured over time and, through mutual trust, the coaching occurs.

The coach—or trusted advisor—provides critical insight and serves as a guiding light to ensure your strategy is correct.

3 PEOPLE

In every business relationship, you should always have at least three people you can call besides your main point of contact. These three people—essentially coaches—will provide a unique perspective on the organization and serve as sources of key information for you on the client.

If you are in sales or sales management, you typically engage and negotiate with a purchasing or supply chain representative. The main goal of these people is to minimize vendors, buy less, and drive the price of the product or service down. Their incentives are not typically aligned with yours.

What about the end user? It is important that they also have a voice.

As part of understanding the buying landscape and how to develop your offering, it is critical you get to know others within the organization. Identify at least three people—ideally in three different geographical or functional areas—and develop a relationship with them to better understand what is important to the organization.

Use their skill, relationships, and knowledge to tailor your offer to meet the needs of the customer. Articulate to them why your product and service solves problems and creates value for their organization.

During the sales process, as you receive feedback from the buyer, work with your three people on what they are hearing internally. Seek feedback on your offer and how it is being perceived. Try to understand if the competition is offering anything unique. Determine ways to make your offer more competitive after identifying the likely factors being considered in the buying process.

Then continue to check in with them as the buying process progresses. The feedback you receive will be critical to your success. And don't forget to thank them. Cultivate those relationships moving forward and know there will be turnover and you will need to develop new relationships with new influencers.

When I was purchasing a home in Florida many years ago, I didn't know the area very well and the real estate agent was somewhat new. The price seemed fair and the house had a lot of promise. But it had been sitting on the market for months without an offer. Something didn't seem right.

I brought in two longtime friends who had substantial remodeling experience. I also brought in a friend who had lived in the town for many years. We found the price had been initially too high and noticed some of the surrounding houses hadn't been remodeled and there was an imbalance in values. I ultimately made a deal at a fair price because I leveraged three additional people not connected directly to the sale.

Another example is the time we had a major contract discussion, and we were told if we didn't agree to a certain price, we would be kicked out of the account. We were certainly concerned, but when we called a couple of the end users, they told us they had no intention to use any other products but ours. The end users strongly advocated for our products and told their management team to make a deal with us.

The account called us and asked us to come in and make a deal. We came to the table with an excellent price and signed a win-win agreement with the customer.

As you assess your sales team, determine if they know at least three people beyond their main point of contact they can call and ask pertinent questions to about the contract situation. Do they have three people programmed in their cell phone they can text or call to get additional insight?

By engaging with three people outside your normal circle, you can take advantage of their skill and knowledge while avoiding overreliance on one person and their view during the negotiation. This separation provides a more balanced perspective and ensures you are in the best position to advance the customer relationship.

GETTING THE CALL

Getting the call means the customer will literally call you and tell you what you need to do to get the business.

In order to get the call, you need to develop a relationship that is so strong that when the customer is ready to decide on who they will partner with, they give you a call.

This means the customer trusts you and wants you to win. If no one calls you, you've probably lost the deal.

We found ourselves in a tough spot with a customer we had spent decades cultivating and strengthening a relationship with. His employer had recently experienced an ownership change, and some competing forces had come on the scene which further displaced the balance of power in his department. As the contract came up for discussion, it was clear we would lose the deal based on price and the volatile environment in the business. However, our champion knew the work of converting our products and the headwinds from the end-users would be a nightmare for his organization to navigate.

Our advocate called us the day before the final decision, telling us we were out unless we modified our offer. While gaining internal support to improve our offer was very challenging, winning the deal made it worth it. Getting the call saved the day.

There are many key factors in getting the call. You must have developed a strong relationship built on credibility and trust. Credibility is built by having the knowledge and understanding of the business (yours and theirs) so you can articulate the value proposition to your customer. You must provide consistent and relevant communication reinforcing the strength of your portfolio and your ability to service their needs.

A strong relationship can be predicated on your ability to create a personal connection with your customer, which includes getting to know the person and developing an authentic and sustainable rapport. However, not all customers are interested in having a personal relationship. That doesn't mean they don't trust you. Remember, it's critical to determine what's important to the customer and provide a solution that meets their needs.

In terms of creating a personal relationship, strive to understand the personality of the customer and what they like. Consider doing research on LinkedIn to discover where they are from, how they built their expertise, and which activities they are passionate about. Look for similarities and connections that can be explored. If someone likes to run or enjoys college football, do some research on those activities or draw from your experiences and integrate them into your conversations. Perhaps they volunteer for an organization supporting at-risk youth, or they are a Den Leader for Cub

Scouts in their community. For me, conversations are natural if the customer loves sports or history.

The customer may prefer exceptional customer service and excellent products. They want to know they can trust your organization to follow through with your commitments and be on time and on target. There is comfort in knowing they can trust you. As the relationship blossoms and trust is created, when the contract comes up for bid, you already know what's important to the customer and can begin showing them the best path: working with you and your organization.

Getting "the call" happens every day in almost every personal and business transaction. When two or more competitors vie for something of value, usually the most likeable, dependable, valuable, and easiest person to deal with wins. Why else would people have insurance agents when it's easy to go online for the best rate? How about money managers? Why not just buy an index fund? Why do we go to the same barber and hairdresser? Hotel chain? Airline?

It is through this relationship-building and development of trust that leads to getting the call. Ask yourself if you have been proactive enough to get the call. If you don't know whether you are getting the call, chances are the competition is getting it.

STAKEHOLDER ENGAGEMENT

Whether you are running a business or leading a team, stay proactive through consistent communication and collaboration with internal stakeholders. This alignment is critical because it ensures you are identifying opportunities to succeed and developing relationships where surprises are kept to a minimum. You shouldn't work as an independent operator. This engagement lets the team know you are working hard to support them and you are actively looking out for their best interests.

I had the pleasure of working with a sales professional who engaged teammates in a way that truly set him apart. He was constantly on his phone and always willing to take your call. He also was ubiquitous. It seemed he was always in the field with customers and the local teams. He was beloved because he was available and maintained a positive attitude.

He also consistently held monthly calls with all his team members to provide an update on his customers, drive communication, and put together actionable plans. Many of his peers would work independently, and while they were effective, inevitably there would be a complaint from an internal stakeholder about a lack of communication.

The benefit of this alignment was it made this phenomenal sales rep invaluable to the local teams when new contracts came up or a customer event happened. They wanted him to be included because he was so good at communicating and helping to accomplish goals. He was simply great at aligning all the stakeholders so his team would win.

DEVELOPING RELATIONSHIPS

Developing relationships refers to the ability to establish rapport with another person, connect with them in a meaningful way, and use that connection to accomplish goals.

Relationships are the true difference maker. If you can develop relationships or you have people who can, you have a decided advantage. Relationships can be built through conversations on mutual interests or by providing dependable service. When people enjoy speaking with or being around other people, they gravitate toward that person and typically want them to win. That is the essence of a relationship.

Charisma, humor, performance, consistency, and reliability are some of the traits that help develop relationships with a client. Whether it is the waiter at the local restaurant, your mailman, your high school friends, or your coworkers, these characteristics are crucial to success.

Being proactive means cultivating those relationships, whether they are personal or business. Show gratitude. Tell the customer and your team why the relationship is important. Strengthen the relationship by delivering even when you don't need to.

Joe De Sena, founder of the popular Spartan race series, has always been highly motivated and driven.[xvii] He personifies proactivity. As he began his entrepreneurial career, Joe developed a pool cleaning business in his teen years. Joe was successful because he did the extra little things to impress his clients and inspire loyalty. Instead of just cleaning the pool, he would straighten the patio furniture and clean up the entire area around the pool. That is how relationships and loyalty are developed. Customer feedback echoed throughout the community and the referral network grew. The interesting part about Joe is that I doubt his clients liked him for his personality and charm. They liked him because he cared and went the extra mile.

I knew a top sales representative who performed extremely well in terms of achieving revenue goals. His ability to develop relationships proved to be priceless. He grew up in his territory—often a key differentiator and huge catalyst to success. He also did the little things that set him apart from his competition.

He raised his own crops, bringing fruit and vegetables to his customers, but with one steadfast and simple rule: they had to pay a modest price. While he was able to cover the cost of his crops, there was an additional intrinsic value. He believed if people paid for the crops, they would be more likely to eat them because of a perceived value. His customers loved him for it. He cared about the plants but was also ensuring his clients received healthy food for a reasonable price.

As you think about your clients and how best to approach them, realize people buy from people they like. The reason for that affinity isn't always personality and charisma. Most customers are drawn to salespeople because of reliability and trustworthiness. As you look at your business and your commercial approach, it is critical you put the right people in place who can develop those critical relationships.

FLY EVERYWHERE—TALK TO EVERYONE

A key to being proactive is having the attitude that you are not afraid to speak with anyone about anything. Get out of the office and meet your internal and external customers. By being present, you will uncover challenges and opportunities you will never see in the office.

One of the best sales representatives I've ever known was an experienced professional with the energy and drive of a recent, highly motivated college graduate. While he's also lovable, funny, genuine, and kind, he has a bit of an edge to him. He wants to win so bad it is borderline humorous. He is driven.

While he is far from perfect, he has a big heart and winning means everything to him. He amazes people with his ability to fly any place, at any time, to speak with anybody. First, he finds the critical person he wants to influence and strives to get close to that person. After developing a relationship, he convinces them his products are the best. He is almost irresistible with his charm and great sense of humor. He uses sports, food—or just a great sense of humor—to draw people in.

Once, we were meeting with a very shrewd and challenging customer. He must have committed some egregious offense that offended her. Standing in the hallway, she started yelling at him, saying how irresponsible and forgetful he was. This went on for some time, and just when I thought he would snap, he looked her in the eye and said, "Merry Christmas." It was November, but we all cracked up. Even the customer began laughing. What a talent.

What also sets him apart is he has relationships in all parts of the country with different customers because he constantly travels throughout the territory to meet people. He is beloved by the local sales teams because of his personality but also his willingness to come to their territory and meet their key influencers. His presence is also non-threatening and fun which alleviates the local team's angst with bringing an outsider into their territory.

And when he makes customer connections, he stays in contact and responds when there are challenges and needs. It became a running joke. Where is he today? How many frequent flier miles does he have? How does his travel budget look?

He won over clients because of his:

- Unmatched drive
- Unique ability to develop quick relationships
- Drive to understand what's important to the customer and deliver
- Non-threatening presence and style
- Amazing customer service
- Customer advocacy
- Unwillingness to say no
- Work ethic
- Caring attitude. He always asks about customers' family and kids—and is sincere. He also speaks lovingly about his kids.

This approach also applies in leadership.

In the Marines, I had the fortune of serving under then Colonel James Mattis—later four-star General then Secretary of Defense—shortly after I returned from my four-month deployment to Somalia as part of Operation Restore Hope. Colonel Mattis assumed command of the 7th Marine Regiment and immediately began implementing his unusual but highly effective leadership style.

In the Marines, every command has an officer of the day and an enlisted Marine who are on site at the Headquarters during the evening—sort of like a night watch—and ensure order and discipline is maintained. This is typically a very uneventful duty calling for both Marines to be available if the phone rings or an incident occurs.

Late at night, both Marines rotate watch, and you can sleep when your partner is at the desk. As I was sleeping late into the night, I was woken by a commotion at the front desk. It was around 2 a.m. on a Sunday and Colonel Mattis was speaking with my partner. I sprang to my feet and addressed him properly.

He responded, "Lieutenant, I'm checking to make sure the building is secure." He then departed. One of the most bizarre but impressive things I witnessed serving in the Marines. The commander was awake in the middle of the night to check on his command to ensure the Marines on guard were vigilant.

You better believe that story got around and everyone knew our leader was always fully invested and expected everyone to do their job . Mattis was sending a message that order and discipline mattered. Even seemingly mundane tasks are important when you are protecting freedom.

This story on Mattis was not an isolated incident. Five years later, General Krulak showed up on Christmas Day to hand out cookies at the large base in Quantico, VA and asked the Marine at the duty desk who the officer in charge was. The Marine answered, "Brigadier General Mattis."

General Krulak thought the Marine misunderstood his question as this duty always went to a very young officer. Brigadier General Mattis suddenly appeared in full uniform, and when asked why he was the officer of the day, Mattis responded the young officer scheduled for duty had a young family and he replaced him so he could spend time with his family. Leadership doesn't get any better than that.[xviii] A general replacing a lieutenant on Christmas Day, sleeping on a cot and performing desk duty on probably the quietest day of the year. I wonder how many CEOs would do that?

By being constantly in the market with customers or walking the floor and engaging with your employees, you will set the tone and show your commitment.

ASK FOR THE BUSINESS

Don't be afraid to make that call and ask the question you want the answer to. What is the worst that can happen? They say no. So. What will happen if you don't ask the question? The answer is definitely no.

I was working with one of my peers and we were speaking to a customer about some new products. In what I perceived as an uncomfortable moment, he asked for her commitment to buy his product. She said yes. Afterward, I told him the situation seemed a little forced and awkward. He looked at me and smiled. He said his father had taught him an important lesson many years ago. The worst that can ever happen when you ask is they say no. You will never make a sale if you don't ask for the business. It has been more than twenty years, and I still remember that moment like it just happened.

When I went to graduate school, one of my classmates told the story of how he had been rejected from the MBA program at the University of Florida. He decided he didn't like that answer, so he made an appointment with the dean of the business school. When asked why he was there, my classmate told the dean he felt like he deserved to be admitted and he would be an asset to the program. The dean let him in.

Whether you are in a sales role and pitching a big deal or you are trying to meet a customer for the first time and can't seem to get through, make the call and ask for the business. If it makes you uncomfortable, keep asking until it becomes natural. This approach is how you maintain proactivity.

SEEK FEEDBACK

I believe it is important to seek feedback from others on your performance and what you can improve on. This critical feedback should be sought from fellow employees and customers. From an employee perspective, ask how you can improve from people who report to you, peers, and your boss. Check in with your customers on a regular basis and ask them how you are doing and what you can improve. Is there anything you can learn from your competition? Other companies?

Whenever I am performing a performance review on one of my direct reports, at the end, I ask them what I can do to better support them. I believe an important part of the review process is a discussion about how the overall employee-supervisor relationship can be improved.

In the 1990s, Home Depot decided to change its return policy to become less restrictive after feedback from customers. The policy became so lenient and customer-centric that the company attracted an even more loyal following. They essentially took returns no matter what condition the item was in. No receipt? No problem.

A friend was working for a store and told me about the time an elderly gentleman brought in a generator that looked like he had dropped it from the top of a ten-story building. The store replaced it without comment. Is there any doubt why Home Depot has been such an amazing success story?

How about the times you have seen the opposite. Think about the times you have witnessed terrible customer service that left a deep impression. There are places I still won't go to because of poor experiences with staff.

Seeking customer and employee feedback is a sure way to drive self-awareness and focus on ways you can improve. It is a gift.

CHAPTER 4: EXCELLING

PREPARATION

Whether it is an internal meeting or one with a customer, have the discipline to prepare for the meeting so there are no surprises and you have a clear agenda and objectives.

Our time is finite, so ensure the time you spend with others is not wasted. Think clearly about what you are trying to accomplish and make a checklist and follow it. At the end of the meeting, do a recap of what was covered, next steps. and identify who has responsibility for each step.

One of my good friends had a meeting with the CEO of one of the largest and most prestigious companies in the world. The CEO was mercurial and extremely intelligent. When my friend sat down, the CEO looked at him blankly and asked him what he wanted. He genuinely seemed confused. My friend was astonished and a bit unnerved. He had never had a meeting like this before. He stumbled through a few sentences, and just when he thought it couldn't get any more uncomfortable, the customer took a phone call and spoke for five minutes, oblivious to my friend. Suffice it to say, that was the last customer meeting with the CEO. He had no plan, and the CEO hadn't been prepped on the meeting.

By being disciplined and preparing for meetings, you will set yourself up for success and ensure you have accomplished or addressed the major topics of interest.

VALUE

Value refers to what the seller or business entity is providing above and beyond just product and price.

In business, there are many value additions businesses can offer. The question is whether they are differentiated or not. Is it something the competition can copy? If so, it really isn't valuable.

Some examples of value-adds include:

- Exceptional service
- Promotions
- Free shipping or free product
- Inventory Management
- Educational programs for customer staff relevant to their job or certification
- Services & Solutions
- Risk share—Allowing payment in the future based on performance standards or committing to a refund (or penalty) for failing to meet performance standards
- Product guarantees
- Discounts for early payment
- Discounts for large orders
- Free replacement of damaged goods

One of the most impressive health executives I have met is a gentleman named Mark Dixon, a consultant and former CEO of Abbott Northwestern

Hospital in Minnesota. Mark does an excellent job of bringing real-world, practical experience and is an expert on hospital C-Suite strategies and value-based healthcare.

Mark spoke about the concept of being a trusted advisor who the customer relies upon to help navigate a complex environment. He described a situation where an account manager with a large company approached him and asked Mark if he could ask him about something outside his normal scope. The account manager said he noticed the floors and walls were dirty and it gave an impression the hospital was not clean and safe. Mark explained to the account manager that patient satisfaction had been lagging, and he was worried about the condition of his facilities.

The account manager then stated he had a colleague at his company who could probably help with the cleaning and for even less money than Mark was currently spending. He facilitated a meeting, and Mark decided to hire the new cleaner. The results were amazing. Marks' floors sparkled, and with that simple solution, his patient satisfaction scores improved dramatically.

What is the point? The supplier was able to develop a deep relationship based on trust because he looked out for the interests of his customer, not just his own. He also leveraged the strength of his company to provide a solution beyond his own interests. He had a customer for life because he was proactive. Twenty years later, Mark was still impressed by the account manager's selfless gesture, and the company always got the nod when contract decisions were made.

I also witnessed value in consumer products in retail. Many suppliers perform inventory counts and replace product on the shelves in grocery stores as part of their service and sales model. This model ensures the product is readily available and any problems like expired or damaged products are minimized. It also provides the supplier an opportunity to sell incremental displays and products during promotions. The stores rely on many of these companies to ensure their shelves are stocked. It is essentially free labor for the stores. The most valuable and differentiated suppliers are the ones with highly committed sales members. They show up early in the morning and during the busiest times—holidays—when the stores are most crowded.

I worked with a gentleman named Dave many years ago who took service to the next level. He showed up on his off days to ensure his product was merchandised correctly. On many occasions, he returned to his stores after a long day servicing his route to restock the shelves. The manager of his largest store loved him, and every time there was a product promotion, Dave got to display his product in the lobby and on displays at the end of the best aisles. He would often get praise from store employees for stocking the shelves with other products when they were low. Eventually, he was even hired by his largest store for peak season hours during his off days. He was a true partner and created value through his commitment to his customers. Dave was proactive.

When you are selling a product or a service, look for ways beyond product features and benefits or price to win the business. Price can be easily matched and defeated.

LEVERAGE RESOURCES

A great way to differentiate is to identify people, programs, and processes that allow you to strengthen your position.

You can be proactive by understanding all the resources you have available and then leveraging them to your advantage.

Resources can be people: your boss, a coworker, a trusted customer who can provide a third-party reference, an expert in your field, or a specialist in your company who can articulate the unique features of your product or service. Think about the people you know who can help you, and then find out how to integrate them into your sales process.

Resources can also be quantitative or qualitative factors. A customer education program or certification courses are examples. It could be a grant to fund a worthy cause, an advertising program, or a sales promotion. How you use these resources is critical as you engage with your customer.

Proactive

I have always been impressed with that rare individual truly able to identify a need and bring all resources to bear. The person who goes the extra mile, asks for the additional favor, stays late when an event ends to thank everyone. The person who remembers your kids' first names and calls you by your first name several times during a conversation. They are proactive.

Some unique examples of creating an exceptional customer experience could include:

- Providing access to a Mercedes during a hotel stay (I had this amazing experience, and it brings us back every year!)
- Providing customized shirts, hats, or tumblers for an event like a reunion or a wedding. It provides a lasting memory and is a personal touch that tells attendees they are special.
- Sending a handwritten thank-you card.
- Calling the competition and securing the customer a substitute for something you don't have.
- Picking up a customer at the airport.
- Follow-up phone call to ensure everything went well.
- Hotels that deliver an umbrella or coffee and donuts in the morning, a champagne toast in the lobby.
- Sending a book to a client after a meeting that touches on something unique that was discussed.
- Sending a dessert with the person's name on it.

One of the best sales representatives at leveraging resources I ever met had an amazing ability to identify what was important and then craft ways to create a customer experience that exceeded expectations. While not the most astute person about the features and benefits of products, he knew how to get people to come to his territory and help him accomplish his goals.

He brought company executives into his territory several times, championed an unprecedented training program, and convinced the CEO to fund a worthy cause for his largest customer. He succeeded because he identified resources that mattered and then worked tirelessly to get people to help him achieve his goals.

The key in effectively leveraging resources is finding what matters to the customer and delivering meaningful value.

THRIVING IN A VIRTUAL ENVIRONMENT

Because of the global pandemic, we are presented with the opportunity to engage our customers in a different way. By becoming an expert in virtual engagement, you can proactively differentiate yourself and ensure that you meet your customer at your best.

Embrace virtual platforms like Zoom and Teams so you can form a personal connection with your customer and your internal team. Seek to understand how your customer likes to communicate and ensure you set up a regular cadence of engagement. Most of these meetings should have a shorter duration and focus on specific objectives.

Always send a short pre-meeting note on objectives, start the meeting by quickly reiterating the purpose, and then get to the point.

In terms of preparation for the meeting, unfortunately virtual meetings take a lot longer to plan. A pre-call with all internal stakeholders is critical as a virtual meeting makes it almost impossible to read body language and communicate non-verbal signals. One important watch-out; don't bring too many internal people to the meeting.

We had a virtual meeting during the global pandemic with a new customer who had a few associates attending that we had never met before. Our team had several people on the call and only a few of them met before the meeting to discuss the strategy. I had been involved peripherally with the customer and the decision had been made to remove me from the situation because we felt the local team could handle it.

Minutes before the meeting was to start, I began receiving urgent text messages indicating that the customer wanted me on the call as did several of the internal stakeholders. We were obviously misaligned and the fact it was a virtual meeting meant I could be summoned at the last minute. I jumped on the call a few minutes late and immediately noticed the awkward silence. I took charge and began presenting to get things moving. After I finished, our team members began presenting their pricing proposals.

While things seemed to be going relatively well—given the circumstances—the customers began questioning us and critiquing many aspects of the offer. As the pressure intensified, one person on our team stated the offer was flexible and we could work with the customer to make the pricing a little more achievable. Gulp. The customer became more aggressive and we began losing control. Because the meeting was virtual, there was no way to signal our teammates before things got out of hand.

It became clear that it was a suboptimal call and we didn't meet the customer's or our objectives. At the end, we hung up and held a separate call where we decided to move forward the best we could. This call reinforced the importance of gaining alignment before the meeting and making sure everyone knew their role and what should be communicated.

Being proactive in the virtual environment is critical. Virtual calls have many positives; you can reach more people, meet more frequently, reduce expenses, and leverage more people internally. However, the virtual environment can be risky. Pre-call planning and discussing roles and responsibilities will ensure you don't get blindsided when you can't read each other's body language. Identify who will speak, and if there is conflict or confusion, make sure you don't make commitments you can't live with.

DIFFERENTIATE

A great way to be proactive is to provide a product or service that is exceptional and can't be copied by the competition. If your product or service is unique and has intrinsic value, customers will want to buy from you.

In the medical technology space, differentiated technology can be a device that allows the physician to more accurately repair the body or the patient to recover more quickly. For example, it could be an artificial hip or knee that can be implanted precisely with a faster recovery time. Another example is a pharmaceutical drug that limits side effects while effectively treating disease.

In consumer products, a wicking material used for workout clothes or a tennis racket with a larger sweet spot are differentiators. A chocolate dessert with low calories or a light bulb that lasts twice as long. Those products demand a premium price.

With the rapidity of technological innovation, the ability to truly differentiate products or services is becoming more challenging. In a highly competitive environment, customers have options. Although hard to admit, some very impressive technology has become a commodity.

Two large orthopedic companies launched new devices almost simultaneously. Both products were innovative, but there was little difference between the two devices, and both were better than the current technology on the market. How do they differentiate?

You must ensure—before the launch—you have thought of every option and how your competitors and customers will react. Relationships, marketing, breadth of portfolio, price—you have many levers you can pull; you just need to pull them more effectively than the competition.

One company achieved better market share. Why? They had prepared better. They conducted quarterly reviews with their customers and brought physician experts into the large cities to speak with the implanting physicians. They tested a few potential deals with customers to see how they would react. Meanwhile, the competition had shown up in their nice suits, very confident they would win because they enjoyed market leadership before the launches. "Well, of course you will select us," they thought. "We are the market leaders."

Conversely, the eventual winners couldn't understand why the competition was so confident. The victors had a much better economic story, and there was little differentiation between the hip implants. The key factor in the victory? The winning company had a proprietary, complementary product used during the procedure, providing the leverage needed to win the deal. The competitor failed to consider this key differentiator. The winner's pitch was very simple: "Our product is as good as our competition's. So, give us that business, and we will make sure you get a discount on our differentiated technology. If you don't give us that business, our proprietary technology will cost you more."

While the competitor also had some unique technology, their only significant levers were relationship and price. If that is all you rely on, the game is over and you will lose.

Customers often have choices. As you think about your offer and how you will compete in the market, position yourself in a differentiated way. Create a product or deliver a service not easily duplicated.

BECOME THE EXPERT

Be a problem-solver. When a fellow employee or customer has a question they must get the answer to, they call you. You accomplish this by becoming the expert. You have knowledge no one else does, and the information is important and relevant. You could be an expert on taxes, health and fitness, buying cars, real estate, or traveling in Europe. If you are an expert in any of those areas, people will want to speak with you.

Have you ever tried to have a pool or fence installed during a pandemic? Good luck. Fence and pool companies were so busy and unable to meet demand during the pandemic because skilled labor from outside the US couldn't come into the country; many US laborers had little incentive to work because of unemployment benefits while demand skyrocketed because people wanted to spend time in their yard. Prices increased dramatically, and timelines for project completion were extended. This environment was ripe for an expert, a person with the skill, team, and access to workers and materials that very few did.

In business, the same rule applies. In the medical space, people are always looking for expertise on reimbursement and the evolution of healthcare. Employees who are experts on those topics are invaluable and highly in demand.

Health systems, insurers, and suppliers need experts on cybersecurity because of how fast technology advances and the risk of security breaches.

These challenges are critically important, and the stakes are worth millions of dollars. And almost no one knows how to address the issue.

Outside of healthcare, niche opportunities exist to excel. Nurses, software developers, mechanical engineers, digital marketing, and teachers are a few of the professions expected to be in high demand in the coming years. [xix]

Identify the knowledge and skills you can obtain that makes you an expert in your field. Put yourself in demand by gaining access to products few can get. Provide a unique service that makes you a highly coveted part of the team or your customer base.

IDEAL

What if you could take the best qualities of the best leaders or sales reps you have ever worked with and create a person. You would be very proactive in business and life. While you can't do that, you can identify those traits and hire and train your team to emulate those qualities.

What if you could create a football player who threw like Tom Brady, ran like Barry Sanders, and blocked like Anthony Munoz? Or an actor who performed like Denzel Washington and sang like Frank Sinatra? Or just take Meryl Streep.

The ideal leader for me starts with someone who has an amazing vision to predict the future. Steve Jobs, Elon Musk, Sara Blakely. That leader would also have high emotional intelligence like Indra Nooyi, Richard Branson, and Warren Buffet; and that leader would have an unmatched drive to win: Jeff Bezos, Michael Jordan, and Tiger Woods.

In term of the best sales professional, they would be:

- Genuine
- Kind
- Charismatic
- Funny
- Empathic
- A Listener

- Collaborative
- Creative
- Driven
- Bright
- A Learner

In most markets, the best sales reps or customer relationship managers are those who have a certain likeability and emotional intelligence that are natural. They don't threaten others by their actions or success, and you are drawn to them. They also have a drive to win that doesn't come across as selfish. They are creative and come up with unique ways to solve problems. They want to get better, and they seek feedback from others. A common thread is many of them have a great sense of humor and are self-deprecating. They laugh at themselves. When you have a tough customer, you want to assign them on that customer because you know they will win.

When you are hiring someone new, think of the traits of highly successful people in your organization, and then try to find a person with many of those same qualities. That is not to say diversity in hiring is bad. Diversity is good and usually the best people are those with diversity of thoughts, experiences, and backgrounds.

What about hiring the best leader or working for the best boss? Think of the qualities that inspire you and make you want to go to work. Are they positive and focused on winning and getting better? Do they have a high sense of accountability and do they listen? Do they seek input from others and have high emotional intelligence? Are they willing to take risks? What experiences do they have that make them different? Would you follow them in tough times, and do you trust them? Do they support you and are they willing to take a stand to defend you?

I have worked for an amazing boss who simply everyone loves. I have known him for a long time, and I have never heard anyone say anything negative about him. Customers, competitors, other employees. How rare is that? When his name comes up in conversations with former coworkers and acquaintances, everyone smiles. When you call him, he always has time for you and makes you feel like you are the center of his focus. And he is highly intelligent and strategic with a great sense of humor. What a powerful package.

The teams he leads have almost no turnover despite demand for his people and the size of the organization. It is leaders like him who build sustained cultures and make companies great. And when you have other leaders in the organization who have opposite traits, the contrast becomes glaring.

No one is perfect, but there are certain characteristics and attributes winners have. Seek to find people with those qualities and hire them or follow them.

CHAPTER 5: MAINTAINING THE EDGE

QUESTION YOUR PATH

Have you ever been comfortable? Complacent? I have. Sometimes it feels nice to keep rolling along in life with few worries. Still, there's that voice in the back of my head telling me something isn't right. It's a sort of sixth sense, a whisper, a quiet plea to get moving and get better.

That's why regular self-assessment is critical. Challenge the status quo and test the foundation of your business and your life. This can come in many forms. Look at your role at work and ask yourself if you are doing everything you can to optimize your approach to the business. Decide if you are in the best job for you and have the right people on your team. Assess your product or service. Is it the best it can be? Have you asked your customers if they are satisfied? What is the competition doing that is differentiated?

How about personally? Are you investing in your career? In yourself physically, emotionally, and spiritually?

It comes down to a simple question. Are you happy and fulfilled in your role, and are you doing everything you can to make your team, company and yourself successful?

One of the best examples of switching course is the story of Apple, which went from being a company of innovation and differentiation in the 1970s and 1980s while introducing a unique personal computer to a financially troubled company that almost failed. Apple suffered several identity crises and stumbled through multiple technology platforms in the 1990s to include digital cameras, appliances, and portable CD players. Several executives, including Steve Jobs, resigned.

When Jobs returned in 1997, the company regained its momentum and launched the iMac the next year, the iPod in 2001, and in 2007 launched the iPhone, which has revolutionized the world. Apple created a paradigm shift in communication and data gathering: a phone with touch screen capability that allows you to play music, videos, and chat with people face to face—quite different from the Mac. In 1997, when Jobs became CEO for the second time, Apple revenues were $7.1B. In fiscal year 2020, Apple revenues were $274.5B.[xx]

What if Jobs had stayed? What if he never came back? Where would Apple be today? How would you be communicating digitally?

How many times have you heard someone say they wish they had done something differently with their lives? I hear it all the time when people learn I served in the Marine Corps. "I wish I had served." "That's the biggest regret I have." In a way, it makes me proud to hear others say that. Also, it's not about who you were and what you did. It's about what you are doing now.

No matter where you are in life, question your path and always look to improve. Be proactive and put in the time and the effort. Don't look backward. Look forward.

WOULD IT MATTER

Would it matter if you weren't in your role? Would it really matter? Could the work be done as well if you weren't there?

It's a tough question, and hopefully one most of us could answer quickly that we make a difference in our role. But if you aren't sure, it should be a good wake-up call that either you need to learn a new skill, become more committed, or get a new job.

There have been times I have taken new roles or switched companies and believed I was irreplaceable. How ridiculous. Each time the company survived.

I have also seen people leave companies and there have been significant challenges afterward. A void was created. The key is making sure your impact as an employee is substantive and can be measured.

The same concept holds for your team. As you assess their performance and fit, ask yourself if performance would suffer if there was a change. Would it improve? How can you best align your team to be even more successful?

To that end, a leader should spend time with their team and develop them so when the leader exits, the team can carry on with success. Ideally, the team is even better after the leader departs.

MIX IT UP

In life and business, if you find yourself and your organization getting stale or complacent, embrace change.

Disruption can be a positive thing. Proactively put people in different positions or try a new way of accomplishing things. If you have been zigging, it's time to zag. If your business is 100 percent online, try a face-to-face approach. If you are focused on growth in a certain geographical region, look at other markets. Explore other applications for your products or services.

The US military has a policy to rotate people every few years into new roles, units, and geographies. The benefit is you get exposed to different jobs like recruiting or working with civilian manufacturers or training others. These experiences broaden your perspective and make you a better professional and person. In addition, you get to experience different styles of leadership. It drives excellence, produces diversity of thought, and avoids complacency. The counterargument is you lose continuity and it can disrupt harmony. I don't buy it.

I am impressed with companies that similarly put people in nontraditional roles to stretch them and the organization. There are companies that elevate HR managers to sales leadership roles. Others move salespeople into marketing and engineers into HR. It is bold and unconventional but makes the organization better and generates a compelling perspective for those lucky enough to experience it. I admire companies and leaders with the temerity and vision to take these bold steps.

The Marine Corps and the Navy SEALs have a tradition of sending some of their best performers to the US Army Ranger School, one of the toughest military courses in the world. What a great idea. You learn from a different branch of military how they are training some of their elite soldiers in an austere, unfamiliar environment. That can only serve to make all branches better through shared experiences and the creation of new skills and knowledge.

I know of another company that took their VP of Human Resources and placed her as a VP of Sales. Bold. They bet on her.

Take the time to look at how you are managing your career and your organization and seek to make changes for the better. Change will lead to some discomfort but ultimately make the organization and you stronger.

ANYTHING IS POSSIBLE

Never. And I mean **never** accept defeat.

Proactive

How often have you felt there was no way you could win? That tough puzzle, climbing a rope, solving a Rubik's Cube, or running a marathon. But if you stay resolute and focus on the task at hand, you can accomplish almost anything.

I had a customer once who, for years, barely even spoke to us. He had been offended by some past transgression from a nameless soul. We kept showing up with a positive attitude. We invited him to educational events and provided training to his staff at will. We kept our cool and maintained our professionalism.

Eventually, he needed a favor, and we were there to provide it. We gladly offered and made sure he got what he needed and didn't ask for anything in return. We were doing our job.

In the end, he came back around. We even got to the point where we could laugh about it. By taking the high road, we were able to move forward, and even if he had never came back, the message you are sending to your team and the customer is you will maintain your professionalism.

Imagine the look on the face of your competition if you show up to their best customer even if you have little or no business. You act professionally and provide service above and beyond what is called for. You lay the foundation for the future. You are proactive.

Sylvester Stallone's life was so hopeless that he had to sell his dog for money to eat. He was offered $125,000 for the script to Rocky but only if someone else could star in it. The offer kept increasing until it hit $360,000, and he still refused. He ultimately accepted a much lower offer so he could star in the film.

Academy Award winner for Best Picture, the 1976 classic *Rocky* tells the story of an ordinary meatpacking worker from Philadelphia, barely literate and with little training or direction, becoming the first fighter ever to go the distance with the champ, Apollo Creed. Creed, the classier and stronger fighter, had no respect and even open disdain for this blue-collar challenger. Round after round, they went back and forth, but Rocky kept getting up, gaining fan support and the respect of the champion. While Rocky didn't win the fight, he won the hearts of his trainer, girlfriend, and the crowd.[xxi] What a wonderful metaphor for his life.

And the story of Rudy Ruettiger, the Notre Dame football walk-on—famous for the 1993 movie *Rudy*—who time and again tried to get on the field only to be told he was too small, too slow, and just not good enough. It is a story of a twenty-five-year-old Navy veteran who only played one game on the gridiron his entire career and proved anything is possible. By refusing to quit and challenging the status quo, Rudy sacked Georgia Tech QB Rudy Allen; the crowd deliriously chanted his name and his teammates carried him off the field.[xxii]

Today, virtually every major college or pro football fan has either seen *Rudy* or heard of it, and they know it is the story of the underdog refusing to quit, no matter the odds.

When facing a tough task, stay focused and determined on the process and the outcome. Like Rocky and Rudy, embrace the challenge and show the resiliency to fight through adversity.

GET UNCOMFORTABLE

One of the best ways to learn is through failure. Try something new that is way out of your comfort zone. The journey will lead to growth spiritually, mentally, and physically. It will make you better.

When I think of a true warrior, I often think of the short life of Marine Corps Major Doug Zembiec. He was a force that appeared and disappeared in a flash, leaving a legacy in his wake. He seemed restless, driven, unsatisfied, and eager to be tested in all aspects of life.

An indefatigable, New Mexico, all-state high school wrestler, he took his talent and zest for life to the wrestling mats of Annapolis, Maryland where he became an all-American at the Naval Academy. Possessed with a seemingly unquenchable thirst for challenges, he sought obstacles and hard work.

Joining the Marine Corps upon graduation from the Academy, The Basic School and Infantry Officers Course followed. Not one to rest on his laurels, he was eventually selected for elite Force Recon training, the most difficult course the Marine Corps offers.

As a company commander in Fallujah in 2004, leading Echo Company 2nd Battalion, 1st Marine Regiment, he was awarded the Purple Heart for wounds received in battle, as well as the Bronze Star for his heroism while personally directing tank fire. Nicknamed the "Lion of Fallujah," in 2007, he was awarded the Silver Star posthumously during his fourth tour of Iraq; this time on special assignment with the CIA.[xxiii]

I often think of Doug Zembiec and believe he sought danger and discomfort. He hunted it. He wanted to feel it. His legend is so large that the Zembiec Award was created to annually recognize outstanding leadership in Special Operations in the Marine Corps.

We can learn from the short but amazing life of Doug Zembiec. Try that new approach to the business. Develop a partnership with a company that can complement your product line. Create a new pricing structure that opens your portfolio to new customers. Implement a radical commercial approach that focuses on a different channel. What do you have to lose?

IMPROVISE. ADAPT. OVERCOME.

When life or business circumstances get complicated, be flexible and look for opportunities to overcome adversity. Proactively attack problems.

A great salesman I know had recently graduated from college and flew into a large city for a round of interviews for a highly coveted sales role with a consumer products company. There were dozens of candidates for only two positions and this young man had taken a late flight, missed his connection and his luggage had been lost.

This is a moment where I would have certainly panicked as he was in a strange city, late at night with an early interview before any clothing stores opened. This clever future salesman noticed an employee in the lobby wearing a tuxedo. He approached him and learned that he was the banquet coordinator and so he offered him $10 to borrow his tuxedo after his shift that night. He then approached a couple of strangers in the lobby that looked like potential candidates and asked if either one had an extra shirt and tie. One nice guy did.

The salesman walked into the interview the next morning with a tight-fitting tuxedo and told the interview panel the story. Guess who got one of the two available jobs?

I heard this story from one of the other candidates at the hotel that morning who said when the salesman walked into the holding room before the interviews and told the story about his tuxedo, he knew that the two jobs available had now become just one. Beautiful.

In business and in sales, look for innovative solutions or different ways to approach a challenge. By improvising and adapting, you can make a seemingly dire situation into a success story.

OWNER

Act like the business is yours. You started it, and you are building it to be great.

There have been many times in my career I have asked myself whether I would tolerate someone's performance if it truly was my company. Unreturned phone calls, rude behavior to customers, sloppy work. If your name was on the building, would you allow that? Then why would you now?

I worked with a phenomenal leader early in my career who told me a story about the first time he arrived at a grocery store as a new sales rep and parked his car as close to the front door as he could. He was laughing as he recalled the story of how the owner started yelling at him as he entered the store.

The store owner said he had started the business decades before so residents could have an affordable and convenient place to shop. He had elderly patrons who had trouble walking, and the last thing he needed was some young sales rep taking a prime parking space because he was too lazy to walk. That story has stayed with me to this day, even when I am shopping at grocery stores, but especially when I see customers. Take a walk.

Act like you own the business you are working for or supporting because if you do, you will expect excellence and go the extra mile. You will be proactive.

THANK-YOU NOTES

Be different. Be memorable. After a meeting with an important client, handwrite them a sincere thank-you letter and mail it to them. Tell them how much you appreciate their time and their business and insert a humorous or personal comment that shows you really know them. It could be something about their child, an upcoming trip they have, or a mutual affection for a specific food.

There was a rep who worked with me many years ago, and she always wrote personal notes and mailed them to me. It made me feel good, and I always associated her with that personal touch. We ran across each other about ten years later, and we had a nice long discussion. I remember thinking immediately of the handwritten notes she had sent. And guess what happened? I received a wonderful card in the mail the following week. Do you think I'll ever forget that? She proactively managed her brand and relationships.

==If you want to stand out and be remembered, take the extra step. Write a thank-you note.==

CHAPTER 6: LEADERSHIP

HARD ON THE ISSUES, NOT THE PERSON

When having discussions on challenging subjects where there are different opinions, focus on the issue and not the person.

Conversations on difficult matters can get emotional. There are often different interests and perspectives. Whether you are talking to an employee, peer, customer, or family member, seek to identify the challenges and focus on a solution.

You can focus on deficits in performance, a lack of progress, and opportunities to improve.

Many leaders are very committed to their jobs but have difficulty with tough conversations. Few people enjoy heated discussions.

I worked with a high-profile leader who was very intelligent and capable; he had no problem sharing his opinions with anyone. In both social and business situations, I noticed he sometimes talked over people, and when he didn't agree with something, he would challenge others while making a "are you kidding me?" or "you're wrong" face. This was surprising because he was a genuinely nice person, and this seemed out of character for him.

After one incident, I observed the look on the faces of his peers. Taking him aside, I asked him how he thought he was perceived by others. He gave me a quizzical look. I told him everyone in the room probably knew he was the smartest one there, and he didn't need to rub it in. He mumbled a bit, and we ended the short discussion. The next day, he took me aside and said no one had ever told him this before, and he was thankful I had.

He's in a different organization now, but countless times since that day, he's mentioned our conversation, thanking me for the direct feedback. He said that while some people might have taken it as too direct or as an attack on their character, he felt fortunate because no one had ever taken the time or interest to point out that shortcoming.

We are all human and want to be treated fairly. If you focus on the issues and the challenges when having tough conversations, you can accomplish great things. Don't focus on what went wrong or why people are doing certain things. Instead, emphasize getting the job done with specific steps to accomplish the objectives. This approach will ensure progress without making it personal.

EAT LAST

As a young Marine officer, I learned an important rule that has always stuck with me. Whether you are leading others, having guests over, or hosting a customer, always eat last.

Why? As a leader or host, you should make sure the team or guests are taken care of first. Be considerate.

I always notice when a leader gets into the line first.

WILL OR WON'T, CAN OR CAN'T

As you reflect on your team and assess their performance, use the concept of will or won't and can or can't.

Determine if they can or can't do the job. Are they capable? Is it possible for them to perform the requirements of the role? Then, ask yourself if they will or won't do it. Do they have the motivation to do the job effectively? Or is the desire not there?

It is a simple test but one that works.

He was a brilliant salesman. The first time I met him, I had just moved to Tampa and he asked me about my real estate agent and how things were progressing with the house hunting. I also knew he was looking for a job on my team. When I told him I had just started looking, he told me to jump in his car, and he spent the next few hours driving me around the area, showing me the best neighborhoods while asking me about my career and my family. I knew I was being sold to, but I still really enjoyed getting to know him. He could sell and he was willing. Will or won't? Will. Can or Can't? Can.

She was very committed and totally invested in the company. She had a tireless work ethic, and I am not sure if I have ever met anyone more positive. However, no matter how much specific information you gave her on a project, she struggled with putting together the pieces and articulating a succinct plan. It was painful. With her attitude, she was willing, but the problem was she can't.

As you think about your people, ask yourself the simple question. Can that person do the job or can't they? An analogy is determining if a person can or can't play in the NBA. Age, experience, skill, and talent are factors in the answer to that question. They may want to play in the NBA, but can they? Most people simply can't because of physical limitations. Similarly, there are people who can't lead a large group of people effectively. Or they can't build a differentiated strategy for a company. That's ok.

There are also people who are willing and who are unwilling. A person may have an incredible amount of talent, but they may not have the desire or passion to do the work. In sports culture, NFL running back Jim Brown retired in the prime of his career at the age of thirty after nine seasons. He had a budding movie career and wasn't thrilled with team ownership. He could have played at a very high level for many years, but he was simply unwilling.

==You may have highly talented employees who don't have the desire to perform, and you may have well-meaning employees who can't perform adequately in the role. The key is ensuring you find people who can do the job and are willing to do the job.==

LEADING BY EXAMPLE

Regardless of the industry or type of role, a leader should always strive to coach their team and teach them how to improve and be successful. One of the most impressive things a leader can do is lead by example. If an employee is struggling with performing their duties, a leader should use their skill and expertise to teach them how. ==If a sales rep is having a hard time selling a new product, the leader should jump in and demonstrate how to do it.==

When I first started in sales, I had an amazing leader who was a great motivator and a fantastic salesman. He was very positive but also very competitive. He worked hard and possessed a passion for the culture of the organization. He also loved challenging his team.

Randomly, he would call me and challenge me to a selling contest. In a single day, we would compete to see who could sell the most product, and whoever won got bragging rights. We would often get to select a partner and go in teams, and we had to verify the total amount sold. It was a little nerve-wracking but also a lot of fun. It has been a long time, but it was the most excitement I have had in selling and my manager was simply great at it.

Another former manager adopted a unique, entertaining selling model when he was a sales trainer. While traveling with his new hires and meeting customers, he challenged them to sell $5,000 a day in new products. One of his creative trainees stood outside the hotel one morning with a sign that stated "$5k or Bust." I love it!

Coaching by example has many positives. First, it shows the employee how, reinforces the strength of the leader and provides a little pressure on the employee to get moving. It is a motivator and a positive reinforcement.

THAT'S THIRTY MINUTES AWAY, I'LL BE THERE IN TEN

This quote from the 1994 film Pulp Fiction is one of my favorites because it speaks to proactivity and making things happen. Actor Harvey Keitel played "The Wolf", a mysterious man who solves problems. When Vincent (John Travolta) and Jules (Samuel L Jackson) find themselves in a dilemma, "the Wolf" drops everything, comes to their aid in an impossible amount of time and takes care of everything. He solves problems.[xxiv]

Adopt this mindset when leading your team and focusing on customer relationships. When your team knows you will drop everything and help them, a deep sense of loyalty and trust is created.

I had a great leader that always answered the phone and was there when I needed him. If I needed him to see a customer, he was there. Discuss a strategy or a tough customer issue? He was there. I didn't need him to do my job, I just needed him to be available. To be ready. To support me.

If I was mad or worried about an issue, he was the voice of reason and the calm in the storm.

As a leader, solve problems. Build trust so that your team calls you when they need help. Be proactive.

HIRE SLOW, FIRE FAST

The success of your organization and the type of culture you create are predicated on who is on your team. Hire great people, and you are likely to be very successful. Hire people who don't work hard and don't get along, you are likely to have major problems. The competition will beat you and customers will abandon you.

As you look to hire, make sure you are very deliberate and you bring several people into the hiring process. Have the candidate speak to employees from several different functional areas if feasible. Some organizations will even have the final candidate meet with customers. Make sure you check references and listen to that voice in your head telling you something is wrong.

In addition, if you have someone on your team who is causing major problems or it is a bad fit, move quickly to replace them. Holding on too long will hurt employee morale, and if the employee is not performing well, surely they can't be happy in the job. Life is too short.

Hiring and replacing employees is arguably the most important part of a leader's role. Having great people will differentiate the company and the team and allow you to compete and win. Conversely, when you have the wrong person on the team, move quickly to replace.

DROP ANCHORS

Culture. Nothing is worse than when you have someone on your team who sucks the air out of the room. The person who is constantly negative or makes sure everyone knows how smart they are. The anchor that weighs your boat down. Develop them or move on.

I knew a leader who always had to have the last word. Whenever I saw him at a meeting or an email popped up, my blood pressure would rise, and I got this sense of foreboding. Meetings were when he really showed his colors. You just knew he was going to make a point to show everyone what he knew or he was going to put someone down. He always made a point to criticize the agenda and direction the company was going. The negativity hung in the air.

We had 360 feedback—an evaluation tool for people to provide specific examples of someone's performance—which revealed his actions were harmful to the culture of the organization. This feedback was provided to his manager and to him. However, he was unable or unwilling to accept the feedback and improve. He ultimately departed the organization and has bounced around since.

You don't want these people in your organization. Drop anchor.

CHAPTER 7: SCENARIOS

KEEPING YOUR BEST EMPLOYEES

One of the worst things a leader faces is when a high-performing employee quits. While we never want to say we have a favorite employee, there's always one who you especially connect to or is a critical cog in the organization you don't quite know if you can live without. Fortunately, life will go on, but it may be painful for a while.

A very talented sales rep I knew dripped with charisma and was able to develop amazing relationships. He had a remarkable knack for making strong personal connections with customers. He was a running enthusiast and quickly identified customers in his territory who ran, holding group runs whenever possible. He enjoyed fishing as well and often took his clients on day trips where he could build better personal connections. He also did a wonderful job of focusing on the staff, holding chili cook-offs and pancake breakfasts to engage them in experiential learning. Brilliant.

But what separated him most was he studied and became an expert in his professional field, artfully explaining why his products should be used instead of the competition's.

He didn't win because of the donuts and pancakes he provided his customers. He constructed binders of data and presentations telling a compelling story supporting his products. He defended his points of view with facts, which reinforced his professionalism and credibility. Then, he practiced and practiced until he knew the story backward and forward. Most important, he believed in his products deeply, becoming incredulous when others disagreed with him.

He was a highly valued employee and had been with his company for decades. However, his manager was promoted, and he didn't "click" with the new manager. Things changed.

His manager had been a good friend, a protector, and his confidante. The competition saw an opportunity. They had lower share and less talented sales reps, and they yearned for a superstar and they would pay the price for an upgrade. The rep's sales performance suffered and his compensation dropped significantly. So, he went to the competition.

How do you prevent this loss? The solution is remarkably simple: Stay close to your best people and invest in them. Never make compensation an obstacle and strive to discover what is important to the employee and double down on it! It doesn't matter if it is praise, money, status, or autonomy; find it and fuel it. Your biggest asset will always be your people, so treat them as such.

WHAT IF THEY LEAVE?

An important part of being proactive is fostering relationships with your internal and external customers so when your sales rep leaves, the business doesn't go with him.

There are several ways you can be proactive in maintaining team stability and cohesion when leading others in sales. A wise boss once gave me some sage advice I will always remember. Develop strong relationships with two or three key clients in every sales territory so that when the sales rep quits or gets promoted, the business doesn't leave with him. Awesome.

I knew a sales representative who lived in a city known to be very hard to break into when you weren't from there. He had signaled to management for a while he was unhappy and even threatened to leave if he wasn't guaranteed his income. He ultimately departed and went to a competitor.

The situation was further exacerbated by the fact that no one else in the organization had strong relationships with any of the key customers.

For the next decade, the sales rep methodically moved vast swaths of business to his new company by leveraging his relationships and skills. He was so entrenched in the community that new competitive reps who came in were very challenged to make an impact.

Think about your team today. What would happen if your best rep left? You are not being proactive if you can't pick up the phone and call the main customers and hold onto the business.

SAYING GOODBYE

No matter why, where, how, or when, make sure your sales rep says goodbye to their customers if he is promoted, quits, or transfers to another territory. No excuses. Demand it and make it happen.

I watched a beloved sales rep take a new role in another city, leaving his territory without saying goodbye or thanking his customers. Worse, he did not stay in touch with most of them.

In an interesting twist, he returned a few years later in a similar role with the competition in the original city. The vitriol and resentment that followed was expected and justified—but no easier to witness. Even years later, some of his closest initial customers refused to speak to him, vowing never to again. And it's hard to blame them.

Sales is an honorable profession, and like all other professions, there will be people with blind spots.

As a leader, step in and ensure your team does the right thing and leaves on a high note. Make sure they say goodbye and celebrate the event. And if you are the sales rep, save yourself some heartache and say thank you and goodbye to your customers.

BEST CUSTOMER MOVES OR ABANDONS YOU

Regardless of the business environment or competitive landscape, cultivate relationships throughout your territory and don't spend all your time and resources on just one customer or account. Ensure your business will always be stable by identifying opportunities to diversify; whether with customers, products, or services.

There is almost nothing more unfair than when things are clicking on all cylinders, you're hitting your sales number, you are on the cusp of another award-winning year, and the unexpected happens; a key customer quits or leaves your territory. He can't wait to tell you the great news; he is moving to Aspen to become a ski instructor. What? Panic ensues, and you're not sure how you will ever succeed in your territory again.

There are also times when a great customer gets upset over things within or outside of your control and he takes it out on you.

Fortunately, life goes on.

Act with integrity and communicate openly with customers. Attempt to address misunderstandings but also acknowledge mistakes. If the customer is still upset, move forward and engage with customers who want to work with you and circle back when things have settled down.

If a customer moves, wish them the best and make sure you stay in contact. They may come back or you may move one day.

Another lesson: diversify your client base just like you diversify your stock portfolio. If one stock goes down, the entire portfolio is not ruined.

CHALLENGING CUSTOMERS

If we could choose our customers, life would be simple and much easier. That is rarely the case. There will be times we face challenging customers who have high expectations that may not be able to be met.

Being proactive entails identifying threats and shaping the environment to mitigate the impact of adverse situations. Sometimes, it involves observing human behavior and looking for a signal something is going wrong.

When selling—and especially in relationship or enterprise management—you always have unexpected challenges. Enterprise management requires as much coordination and collaboration with your internal stakeholders as it does with your customers. If you don't fully align with your internal customers, your progress with external customers will be jeopardized.

I remember a tough customer I dealt with many years ago. The relationship was so weak the customer awarded a contract to another supplier without going through a bidding process. That's like choosing sides for a pick-up basketball game and leaving a player unselected. Not good.

There were many signs things weren't going well. Every time we met with the customer, there was tension in the room. We had also experienced a lot of turnover in our customer relationship team. Finally, we had a reputation for not handling losses well. The local sales team would cause problems, creating friction for everyone.

Many of our leaders felt we were wasting time by engaging with the customer. The sales team was skeptical the customer would ever choose us. The customer felt we would never be able to provide enough financial incentives to switch.

We faced many challenges: a defensive customer, distrust, and internal stakeholders who felt the relationship wasn't worth our time.

The account manager knew the key was to develop a meaningful relationship with the customer and prove our products, people, and programs could provide a benefit. He made several tactical and strategic moves to begin the establishment of trust. He set up several leadership meetings aimed at developing credibility and internal support for the customer. Concurrently, he held several meetings with the local sales teams and charged them with identifying key players throughout the customer's regional offices. He partnered with the sales team on product messaging and coordinated their activities in the market.

The account manager did an amazing job of meeting the customer's needs. The sales reps did their job, and the financial offer was substantial. When the final calculation was made, the relationship manager had proactively ensured every potential challenge was addressed internally and with the customer.

When the contract decision was made, it wasn't even close.

When you have tough customers, it may be time for a reset. Reset the relationship. Reset your expectations. Reset your approach. Bring in a new relationship manager and brainstorm on ways you can do things differently. You may even consider changing your entire commercial approach with the customer. Double down on even more resources or completely pull away if you have the ability. Consider making the customer a house account covered by inside sales. Develop a proactive approach to win or mitigate the pain.

NEW ENTRANT IN THE MARKET

No matter how mature or competitive a market is, disruption is always a challenge. This is especially true when the incumbents are unaware and unprepared. The case for preparation is evident and there are several ways to alleviate the impact—or preempt the entry.

As the market leader, be present and active with your customers, understand their needs, and seek to fill any gaps in your product line. Seek to understand the competitive landscape and what potential areas of focus the competition is centered on.

The entry of Japanese carmakers into the US in the 1970s and 1980s proved disruptive. These highly efficient, visually appealing, and dependable cars were offered at better prices than the legendary US brands.

How about Tesla? Founded in 2003 and named after Thomas Edison's rival, Nikola Tesla, the company promised electric cars that would revolutionize the car industry. Tesla would bring to fruition the promise offered initially by GM's electric car, EV1, in test markets in the mid and late 1990s.

In 2004, Elon Musk invested $30 million, joining the company as chairman of the board. Tesla's 2008 Roadster overcame many challenges traditional electric cars had faced, offering a powerful enough engine while delivering a meaningful battery life.

Tesla had a tumultuous start but successfully launched three car versions that have decreased in price over time, even while its stock and cash flow fluctuated dramatically. Elon Musk has charismatically and controversially steered the company through the many storms, and today the electric vehicle is the future.[xxv]

The advent—and eventual adoption—of electric cars was inevitable. The value proposition is real: better for the environment and cheaper to operate. If you can get battery capacity improvements and continue to drive costs down, shouldn't all cars be electric?

From a global perspective, the United States and other countries will reduce reliance on foreign oil and pollution will be mitigated.

And to think Ford, GM, Chevrolet, Toyota, and Honda didn't see this? Why weren't they more proactive? Why didn't they invest in their own electric platforms many years before Tesla and even as the Tesla brand grew? Musk even tweeted that he offered Apple CEO Tim Cook the opportunity to acquire Tesla at 1/10 its current price as of December 2020.[xxvi]

Make sure you are constantly evaluating your business position and environment so you can proactively deal with threats. By seeing these threats before they become too powerful, you can implement a strategy that ensures your survival and even makes you more productive and profitable.

LOSING

Sometimes, losing a deal is ok. Losing can be a great teacher. You learn how you could have approached the situation differently, and it will prepare you to better deal with future opportunities and challenges.

We had enjoyed a long and mutually beneficial partnership. The new competitive product was simply better. As we approached our two-year contract with this customer, we knew we faced some big challenges.

We had discontinued an older product while launching an unproven (but potentially better) product just before the contract negotiation. The customer had also been experiencing some transformational changes, bringing on new stakeholders very focused on costs. Further complicating our position was the competition had much more flexibility on pricing as their margins were superior—this would prove difficult to overcome in a highly price-sensitive market.

We had many historical relationships and a strong portfolio, but it was an uphill battle. The competition's value proposition was clearly superior. It should have been obvious we would lose.

We could have focused on other products or lobbied internally for a lower price to match the competition, but it likely wouldn't have mattered. Our biggest supporter was tired of supporting us, the competition had a great product, and they had more pricing flexibility. Case over.

At times, bad things will happen no matter how proactive you are. The key is preparing as much as possible but know you will face adversity.

If the approach or function of the product isn't working, do your best to improve the situation. However, put a deadline on success. If you don't meet that deadline, move on. If you have a client you have been calling on and you continue to hit roadblocks, try a different approach. If progress is not made, it's time to focus elsewhere.

FINAL THOUGHTS

Proactivity is the key to achieving excellence in developing teams, achieving goals and building lasting customer relationships.

Being prepared for challenges in business means having situational awareness and adopting a proactive approach. Seek to influence your environment through action and accountability. This mentality will ensure you are ready for anything.

Because challenges will occur.

Do everything in your power to positively influence customer relationships so they have no desire to explore other options. Show them qualitative and quantitative proof of why they should stay with you.

Reinforce the strength of your relationship by conducting quarterly business reviews. Focus on the customer and identify mutual interests and objectives then consistently measure and communicate goal achievement.

The people you hire and retain on your team ultimately will decide whether you are successful or not. Focusing on an improvement mindset where you coach and motivate others is critical. While the competition will also try to win, differentiate by owning your journey, questioning your path, and getting uncomfortable.

When you become proactive, the decisions you make and the actions you take will put you in a position to consistently improve and drive success. If you have discipline and make principled decisions, the world is in your hands. Enjoy the journey.

Checklist

In Business/Sales/Customer Relationships

Team Planning:

- Do you have a business plan?
- Is it reviewed monthly?
- Does it include objectives and steps to achieve them?
- Did your team develop the objectives?
- Are they SMART? Specific, Measurable, Actionable, Relevant and Time-bound?

Communication:

- Are you performing QBR's?
- Have you asked the customer what their priorities are and what they want to accomplish before the QBR?
- Are the goals of the relationship clearly stated and do they achieve mutual interests?
- Did you do research on the customer and identify something relevant for the discussion?
- Are you using analytics to reinforce the benefit of your product or service?
- Have you kept internal stakeholders updated on the relationship and received their input?
- Did you identify actions items at the end of your meeting and follow-up with an email/written note?

Differentiation:

- Have you developed a customer coach? How are they helping you?
- Are you getting the call when the decision is being made?
- Are you going above and beyond?
- Can the competition copy you? Is your value differentiated? If not, make it differentiated

- Have you engaged every key decision-maker? Internal and external?
- Have you challenged the status quo?
- Have you questioned your path? Is there a better way?
- Have you asked yourself "What If?"
- Are you listening to that voice in your head? Is something not right?

ABOUT THE AUTHOR

Will Gray has more than twenty-five years of sales, marketing and leadership experience with Fortune 500 companies. He served as an officer in the Marine Corps including a deployment to Mogadishu, Somalia in support of Operation Restore Hope. He holds a BA in History and an MBA with a focus in Management and Entrepreneurship from the University of Florida. Although a third generation Floridian, he now lives in Concord, MA with his family and can be contacted at willgrayproactive@gmail.com.

ENDNOTES

[i] https://nordstromcompanyanalysis.weebly.com/vission-and-mission.html

[ii] https://www.amazon.jobs/en/working/working-amazon

[iii] https://thewaltdisneycompany.com/about/#:~:text=The%20mission%20of%20The%20Walt,the%20world's%20premier%20entertainment%20company

[iv] Lencioni, Patrick M. 2002. HBR Make Your Values Mean Something.

[v] https://www.marriott.com/culture-and-values/core-values.mi#

[vi] https://www.kelloggcompany.com/en_US/our-values.html

[vii] https://www.salesforce.com/company/about-us/

   [viii] https://www.cbinsights.com/research-CBI-company-culture (Shouldn't be indented)

[ix] https://campminder.com/culture/

[x] Wilde, Robert. 2018. The Maginot Line: France's Defensive Failure in World War II Maginot Mentality.

[xi] Doerr, John. *Measure What Matters: How Google, Bono, and the Gates Foundation Rock the World* with OKRs. (New York: Portfolio/Penguin, 2018), 27-51

[xii] Doran, George, Arthur Miller, James Cunningham. 1981. "There's a SMART way to write management goals and objectives." (Management Review, 1981), 35-36

[xiii] https://www.impaxcorp.com/

[xiv] Van Horne, Patrick, and Jason Riley. 2014. *Left of Bang: How the Marine Corp's Combat Hunter Program Can Save Your Life.* (New York: Black Irish Entertainment LLC, 2014).

[xv] McDermott, Annette. 2018. "How 'Deep Throat' Took Down Nixon From Inside the FBI." https://www.history.com/news/watergate-deep-throat-fbi-informant-nixon.

[xvi] West, Owen. 2012. *The Snake Eaters.* (New York: Simon & Schuster Paperbacks,

2012)

[xvii] Sena, Joe De. *Spartan Up!: A Take-No-Prisoners Guide to Overcoming Obstacles and Achieving Peak Performance in Life.* 24. (Boston: Houghton Mifflin Marcourt, 2014), 24

[xviii] Le, Vanna. 2018. "Jim Mattis once pulled Christmas duty for a young Marine—and it's the perfect holiday story." https://www.cnbc.com/2018/12/21/why-jim-mattis-once-pulled-christmas-duty-for-a-young-marine.html.

[xix] Kiersz, Andy and Madison Hoff. "The 30 Best High-Paying Jobs of the Future." *Business Insider.*

[xx] MacRumors Staff. 2020. "Apple Reports 4Q 2020 Results: $12.7B Profit on $64.7B Revenue." https://www.macrumors.com/2020/10/29/apple-4q-2020-results/.

[xxi] Ward, Tom. 2017. "The Amazing Story of the Making of 'Rocky.'" https://www.forbes.com/sites/tomward/2017/08/29/the-amazing-story-of-the-making-of-rocky/?sh=5a635d8d560b.

[xxii] McGee, Ryan. 2019. "The story of Notre Dame icon Rudy Ruettiger? It's almost too good to be true." https://www.espn.com/college-football/story/_/id/28231473/the-story-notre-dame-icon-rudy-ruettiger-almost-too-good-true.

[xxiii] Gibbons-Neff, Thomas. 2014. "Legendary Marine Maj. Zembiec, the 'Lion of Falluja,' died in the service of the CIA." https://www.washingtonpost.com/world/national-security/iconic-marine-maj-zembiec-the-lion-of-fallujah-died-in-the-service-of-the-cia/2014/07/15/71501d2c-0b77-11e4-8c9a-923ecc0c7d23_story.html.

[xxiv] https://www.miramax.com/movie/pulp-fiction/

[xxv] Reed, Eric. 2020. "History of Tesla: Timeline and Facts." https://www.thestreet.com/technology/history-of-tesla-15088992.

[xxvi] Kolodny, Lora. 2020. "Elon Musk says he once considered selling Tesla to Apple, Tim Cook didn't want to take a meeting." https://www.cnbc.com/2020/12/22/elon-musk-pondered-sale-of-tesla-to-apple-says-tim-cook-wouldnt-meet.html.

Made in the USA
Coppell, TX
07 July 2023